cont

British & North American Readers:
Please note that Australian cup and
spoon measurements are metric. A quick
conversion guide appears on page 63.
A glossary explaining unfamiliar terms
and ingredients begins on page 60.

2 pulses and grains

Beans, peas and lentils (collectively known as pulses) that need soaking, should be covered with cold water for a maximum of 8 hours; they may ferment if soaked for longer. Then, they should be drained, rinsed (they can be frozen at this stage), put into a large pan, covered with cold water, brought to the boil, and simmered, uncovered, for the required cooking time.

barley, pearl
The outer husk (bran) has been removed and the grain has been steamed and polished. No need to soak, pearl barley will cook in 30 minutes.

black-eyed beans
Small kidney-shaped beans, cream-coloured, with little black markings, like eyes. Soak them overnight and cook for about 30 minutes.

borlotti beans
Large kidney-shaped beans, beige to brown with dark red speckles that disappear when cooked. Soak beans overnight and cook for about 1 1/2 hours.

top row from left:
pearl barley;
black-eyed beans;
borlotti beans;
kidney beans.

second row from left:
pinto beans; burghul;
chickpeas; lentils.

third row from left:
polenta; arborio rice;
basmati rice;
brown rice.

bottom row from left:
white rice; wild rice;
yellow split peas; green
split peas.

kidney beans
Dark red kidney-shaped beans. Soak overnight, boil for 10 minutes, then cook for about 30 minutes.

pinto beans
These are like small borlotti beans. Soak overnight and cook for about 1 1/4 hours.

burghul
Also called cracked wheat and bulghur. To cook, pour boiling water over it, stand for 15 minutes; drain well.

chickpeas
Also called garbanzo beans or ceci, soak overnight and cook for about 1 hour.

lentils
Red lentils do not require soaking. Cook for about 10 minutes. Soak brown (also called green) lentils overnight and cook for about 45 minutes.

polenta
Also known as cornmeal. It is cooked in boiling water or milk for about 20 minutes and eaten as it is, or spread out to dry, cut into shapes and fried.

arborio rice
Large round-grained rice that absorbs liquid without turning too soft. It is perfectly suited to risottos and takes about 35 minutes to cook.

basmati rice
A thin, white, fragrant, long-grained rice; wash it before cooking. It cooks in about 15 minutes.

brown rice
Cook brown rice for about 30 minutes.

white rice
Available in long and medium (known as short) grain. Cook for about 15 minutes.

wild rice
Actually a seed from an aquatic grass. It has a nutty flavour and chewy texture. Cook for about 30 minutes.

split peas
No need to soak. Yellow split peas cook in about 30 minutes; green peas take about 1 1/2 hours.

Vegetable stock

4 bay leaves

2 large (360g) carrots, chopped

2 large (360g) parsnips, chopped

4 medium (600g) onions, chopped

12 sticks celery, chopped

2 teaspoons black peppercorns

6 litres (24 cups) water

Combine all ingredients in large pan, simmer, uncovered, 1 1/2 hours; strain.

Stock can be refrigerated after cooking, then frozen in batches for up to 6 months.

Makes about 2.5 litres (10 cups).

capsicum casserole
with zucchini and beans

$^1/_2$ cup (100g) dried borlotti beans
4 medium (800g) red capsicums
4 medium (480g) zucchini, chopped
4 (100g) baby onions, quartered
200g green beans, halved
300g can chickpeas, rinsed, drained
$^1/_4$ cup (20g) flaked parmesan cheese

tomato sauce
2 x 400g cans tomatoes
1 tablespoon balsamic vinegar
$^1/_2$ teaspoon sugar
$^1/_4$ cup shredded fresh basil leaves

Cover beans with cold water in medium bowl; stand, covered, overnight.
Drain beans; add to large pan of boiling water, boil, uncovered, about
20 minutes or until tender; drain.
Halve capsicums lengthways, remove seeds and membranes. Place
capsicums, cut side up, in shallow 3 litre (12-cup) heatproof dish.
Combine borlotti beans, zucchini, onions, green beans and chickpeas in
bowl, mix well; spoon into capsicums, pour over Tomato Sauce. Bake,
covered, in moderate oven 1 hour, remove cover, bake about 15 minutes
or until capsicums are tender. Serve topped with cheese flakes.
Tomato Sauce Combine undrained crushed tomatoes, vinegar and sugar
in pan, simmer, uncovered, about 5 minutes or until sauce is slightly
thickened. Stir in basil.

Microwave Suitable
Per serve fat 4g; fibre 16g; kj 1009

vegetable and split pea
sambar

1/2 cup (100g) yellow split peas

cooking-oil spray

1 medium (150g) onion, sliced

2 teaspoons ground ginger

1 teaspoon ground cumin

1 teaspoon ground coriander

1/2 teaspoon ground turmeric

3 cardamom pods, bruised

4 curry leaves

400g can tomatoes

1/4 cup (15g) shredded coconut

2 teaspoons brown sugar

2 teaspoons tamarind concentrate

2 teaspoons yellow mustard seeds

500g tiny new potatoes, halved

1 small (250g) kumara, chopped

1 medium (120g) carrot, chopped

2 medium (240g) zucchini, chopped

1/4 cup (60ml) water

2 teaspoons lime juice

Place split peas in medium bowl, cover with cold water, stand 1 hour; drain.

Heat large pan, coat with cooking-oil spray, add onion, cook, stirring, until lightly browned. Add all the spices and curry leaves, cook, stirring, until fragrant.

Blend or process undrained tomatoes, coconut, brown sugar, tamarind and mustard seeds until pureed.

Add split peas and tomato mixture to onion mixture in pan, simmer, covered, 10 minutes. Add potatoes, kumara and carrot to same pan, simmer, covered, 15 minutes. Add remaining ingredients, simmer, covered, 10 minutes or until vegetables are tender.

Per serve fat 5g; fibre 11g; kj 1169

rice and pumpkin
quiche

You will need to cook about ³/₄ cup (150g) brown rice for this recipe.

cooking-oil spray

2 cups cooked brown rice

1 egg, beaten lightly

¹/₄ cup (25g) packaged breadcrumbs

¹/₄ teaspoon dried mixed herbs

pumpkin filling

500g pumpkin, peeled, chopped

2 eggs, beaten lightly

¹/₂ cup (125ml) skim milk

125g smoked cheese, grated

Coat 20cm pie plate with cooking-oil spray. Combine rice, egg, breadcrumbs and herbs in bowl; press mixture over base and side of prepared plate. Bake in moderate oven 15 minutes.

Spoon Pumpkin Filling over base, bake in moderate oven 30 minutes or until set. Serve sprinkled with chopped fresh parsley, if desired.

Pumpkin Filling Boil, steam or microwave pumpkin until tender, drain and mash. Combine eggs, milk and cheese in medium bowl, add pumpkin; mix well.

Microwave Pumpkin suitable
Per serve fat 17g; fibre 3g; kj 1663

lentil and kumara
parcels

Boil, steam or microwave silverbeet until just wilted, rinse under cold water, drain; pat dry on absorbent paper.

Combine water, onions and garlic in pan, cook, stirring, until onions are lightly browned. Add lentils, seeds and extra water, simmer, covered, stirring occasionally, 45 minutes or until lentils are soft and liquid is absorbed. Add more water if necessary during cooking. Stir in kumara; cool.

Divide lentil mixture among silverbeet leaves. Fold in sides of leaves, roll up to enclose filling. Place parcels into top half of steamer, steam over boiling water about 8 minutes or until filling is heated through. Serve with Tomato and Cumin Sauce.

Tomato and Cumin Sauce Blend or process tomatoes and cumin until smooth; strain. Place strained mixture in pan, stir over heat until hot.

You will need to cook 1 medium (400g) kumara for this recipe.

8 silverbeet leaves

2 tablespoons water

2 medium (300g) onions, chopped finely

2 cloves garlic, crushed

3/4 cup (150g) brown lentils

1 1/2 teaspoons cumin seeds

3 cups (750ml) water, approximately, extra

1 1/3 cups cooked mashed kumara

tomato and cumin sauce

400g can tomatoes

1 teaspoon ground cumin

Per serve fat 1g; fibre 14g; kj 894

pumpkin lasagne

500g butternut
pumpkin, chopped

1 teaspoon olive oil

1 medium (150g)
onion, chopped

1 clove garlic, crushed

1 teaspoon sugar

1 tablespoon dry
white wine

9 instant lasagne
pasta sheets

3/4 cup (150g) low-fat
ricotta cheese

3/4 cup (75g) grated
low-fat mozzarella
cheese

1/2 cup (60g) grated
low-fat cheddar cheese

tomato sauce

2 teaspoons olive oil

1 medium (150g)
onion, chopped

1 clove garlic, crushed

2 teaspoons sugar

1 tablespoon chopped
fresh basil leaves

2 teaspoons cracked
black pepper

2 x 400g cans
tomatoes

Per serve fat 13g;
fibre 7g; kj 1653

Boil, steam or microwave pumpkin until soft; drain, mash. Heat oil in pan, add onion and garlic, cook, covered, until onion is soft. Add sugar and wine, cook, stirring, until almost all the liquid has evaporated. Stir onion mixture into pumpkin; mix well.

Place 3 lasagne sheets into greased shallow 2 litre (8-cup) heatproof dish. Spread with half the pumpkin mixture, half the ricotta, then a third of the Tomato Sauce. Repeat layers, ending with remaining lasagne sheets and remaining Tomato Sauce; sprinkle with combined mozzarella and cheddar cheeses. Bake in moderate oven 30 minutes or until pasta is tender.

Tomato Sauce Heat oil in pan, add onion and garlic; cook, covered, over low heat until onion is soft. Add sugar, basil, pepper and undrained crushed tomatoes. Simmer, covered, about 20 minutes or until sauce is thickened slightly.

lettuce parcels

11

with carrot sauce

5 medium (1kg) potatoes

1 medium (120g) carrot, grated

2¹/₂ cups (200g) shredded cabbage

1 tablespoon water

2 medium (300g) onions, chopped

2 cloves garlic, crushed

³/₄ cup (90g) grated low-fat cheddar cheese

1 tablespoon sunflower seed
kernels, chopped

1 tablespoon linseeds

2 tablespoons chopped fresh parsley

2 tablespoons chopped fresh
coriander leaves

8 iceberg lettuce leaves

carrot sauce

3 medium (360g) carrots

2 cups (500ml) water

1 large vegetable stock cube

Boil, steam or microwave potatoes until tender; drain. Mash potatoes in large bowl. Boil, steam or microwave carrot and cabbage separately until tender, drain, add to potato mixture in bowl; mix well.

Combine water, onions and garlic in small pan, cook, stirring, until onions are soft and water has evaporated. Add to potato mixture with cheese, kernels, linseeds and herbs; mix well.

Drop lettuce leaves into large pan of boiling water, drain immediately, rinse under cold water; pat dry on absorbent paper, being careful not to tear the leaves. Divide potato mixture among leaves, roll up firmly. Serve with hot Carrot Sauce.

Carrot Sauce Slice carrots, combine with water and crumbled stock cube in pan, simmer, covered, about 20 minutes or until carrots are very soft. Blend or process carrot mixture until smooth.

Microwave Suitable
Per serve fat 4g; fibre 12g; kj 1124

12 rice and zucchini
patties

Combine rice,
zucchini, onion,
parsley, pepper, eggs,
breadcrumbs and
corn in bowl; mix well.
Shape mixture into
12 patties. Heat non-
stick pan, coat with
cooking-oil spray,
cook patties, in
batches, until
browned both sides
and heated through.

*You will need to cook about 2/3 cup (130g)
brown rice for this recipe.*

1¹/₂ cups cooked brown rice

3 medium (360g) zucchini, grated

1 medium (150g) onion, chopped finely

1 tablespoon chopped fresh parsley

2 teaspoons seasoned pepper

2 eggs, beaten lightly

1 cup (70g) stale breadcrumbs

130g can creamed corn

cooking-oil spray

Freeze Cooked patties
suitable
Per serve fat 5g; fibre 5g;
kj 1061

mixed vegetable
chow mein

5 Chinese dried
mushrooms

350g packet thin fresh
egg noodles

1 teaspoon sesame oil

cooking-oil spray

3 cloves garlic,
crushed

1 tablespoon grated
fresh ginger

1 small fresh red chilli,
chopped finely

1 medium (120g)
carrot, sliced

2 sticks celery, sliced

125g snow peas,
sliced

1 small (400g)
Chinese cabbage,
shredded

425g can baby corn,
drained, sliced

2 teaspoons cornflour

1/4 cup (60ml) water

1 cup (250ml)
vegetable stock

2 teaspoons soy
sauce

1 tablespoon hoi sin
sauce

6 green onions, sliced

Place mushrooms in heatproof bowl, cover
with boiling water, stand 20 minutes. Drain
mushrooms, discard stems, chop caps finely.
Rinse noodles under cold water; drain.
Combine noodles with sesame oil in bowl. Heat
wok or large pan, coat with cooking-oil spray,
add noodles, stir-fry 2 minutes or until heated
through, remove.
Heat same wok or large pan, coat with cooking
oil-spray, add garlic, ginger, chilli, mushrooms,
carrot and celery, stir-fry until carrot is just
tender. Add snow peas, cabbage and corn, stir-
fry until cabbage is just wilted. Add blended
cornflour and water, stock and sauces, stir over
heat until sauce boils and thickens slightly. Add
noodles and onions, stir until heated through.

Per serve fat 4g; fibre 8g; kj 1035

14 spinach and ricotta
crepes

½ cup (75g) plain flour

2 eggs, beaten lightly

1 tablespoon vegetable oil

¾ cup (180ml) skim milk

filling

250g packet frozen spinach, chopped

1¼ cups (250g) low-fat ricotta cheese

¼ teaspoon ground nutmeg

tomato sauce

1 cup (250ml) tomato pasta sauce

¼ teaspoon dried basil leaves

2 teaspoons cornflour

¼ cup (60ml) dry white wine

Sift flour into bowl, gradually whisk in combined eggs, oil and milk, whisk until smooth. Cover; stand 30 minutes.

Pour 2 to 3 tablespoons of batter into heated, greased, heavy-based crepe pan. Cook until lightly browned underneath; turn, brown other side. Repeat with remaining batter.

Spoon warm Filling onto half of each crepe, fold into triangles and place in shallow heatproof dish. Bake, covered, in moderate oven about 15 minutes or until heated through. Top with Tomato Sauce.

Filling Place spinach in medium pan, stir over heat until all liquid has evaporated. Remove from heat, stir in cheese and nutmeg; mix well.

Tomato Sauce Combine pasta sauce, basil and blended cornflour and wine in pan. Cook, stirring, until sauce boils and thickens slightly.

Per serve fat 14g; fibre 5g; kj 1285

16 curried chickpea
salad

3 x 300g cans chickpeas, rinsed, drained

1 small (100g) red onion, chopped finely

1 large (600g) mango, chopped finely

1 medium (150g) apple, peeled, chopped

1 tablespoon chopped fresh mint leaves

1 tablespoon chopped fresh coriander leaves

$1/4$ cup (15g) shredded coconut, toasted

dressing

$3/4$ cup (180ml) low-fat yogurt

3 teaspoons mango chutney

1 clove garlic, crushed

2 teaspoons mild curry powder

1 tablespoon lime juice

Combine all ingredients with Dressing in bowl; mix well.
Dressing Combine all ingredients in bowl.

Per serve fat 6g; fibre 10g; kj 1130

spinach, potato and fetta cheese pie

2 medium (400g)
potatoes, peeled

2 tablespoons water

1 medium (350g) leek,
sliced

1 clove garlic, crushed

1/2 teaspoon cumin
seeds

2 bunches (1kg)
English spinach,
shredded

100g reduced-fat fetta
cheese, crumbled

1 tablespoon chopped
fresh dill leaves

2 large (700g) red
capsicums

4 sheets fillo pastry

cooking-oil spray

Grease deep 19cm square cake pan. Cut potatoes into 1cm pieces. Boil, steam or microwave until tender, rinse; drain.

Combine water, leek, garlic and cumin in non-stick pan; cook, stirring, until leek is soft. Gently stir in potatoes; cool. Boil, steam or microwave spinach until just wilted; drain well. Toss with fetta and dill.

Quarter capsicums, remove seeds and membranes. Roast under grill or in very hot oven, skin side up, until skin blisters and blackens. Cover with plastic or paper for 5 minutes, peel.

Layer 2 sheets of pastry in prepared pan, spraying each with cooking oil. Fold in long side to fit base; allow excess to overhang each side. Repeat with remaining pastry, covering two other sides of pan.

Spoon spinach mixture over base, cover with capsicum, then potato mixture.

Fold in pastry to cover top. Spray with cooking oil, bake in hot oven 30 minutes or until browned.

Per serve fat 6g;
fibre 9g; kj 1021

18 black-eyed bean soup
with pinwheel damper

1 cup (200g) dried black-eyed
beans

1 tablespoon reduced-fat margarine

2 medium (300g) onions, chopped

2 medium (240g) carrots, chopped

1 small (250g) kumara, chopped

1 medium (125g) turnip, chopped

2 sticks celery, chopped

2 medium (240g) zucchini, chopped

2 x 400g cans tomatoes

2 cups (500ml) water

1 large vegetable stock cube

2 teaspoons tomato paste

pinwheel damper

1 tablespoon reduced-fat margarine

12 green onions, chopped

1/2 cup chopped fresh parsley

2 cups (300g) white self-raising
flour

1 cup (160g) wholemeal
self-raising flour

2 teaspoons sugar

1/2 cup (125ml) skim milk

2/3 cup (160ml) water,
approximately

1 egg white, beaten lightly

Cover beans with cold water in large bowl; stand, covered, overnight.

Drain beans. Heat margarine in pan, add onions, carrots, kumara, turnip and celery, cook, stirring, 5 minutes. Add beans, zucchini, undrained crushed tomatoes, water, crumbled stock cube and paste. Simmer, covered, about 45 minutes or until beans are tender. Serve with Pinwheel Damper.

Pinwheel Damper Heat margarine in small pan, add green onions and parsley, cook, stirring, for 1 minute; cool.

Sift flours and sugar into bowl, stir in milk and enough water to make a sticky dough. Turn dough onto floured surface, knead gently until smooth. Divide mixture in half, roll each half to a 20cm x 30cm rectangle, spread both rectangles with green onion mixture. Roll up both rectangles from long side. Cut each roll into 6 slices.

Place slices, cut side up, into 2 x 17cm round sandwich cake pans, brush tops with egg white. Bake in hot oven about 15 minutes or until well browned.

Per serve fat 8g; fibre 27g; kj 2894

20 quick cheesy spinach
pizzas

2 bunches (1kg) spinach, roughly chopped

140g tub pizza sauce

2 tablespoons tomato paste

2 cloves garlic, crushed

300g button mushrooms, sliced

4 large wholemeal pitta bread

1 cup (200g) low-fat ricotta cheese, crumbled

2/3 cup (80g) grated low-fat cheddar cheese

2 tablespoons (25g) pine nuts

Add washed spinach to dry pan over low heat, stir until wilted; drain, pat spinach dry with absorbent paper.

Combine pizza sauce, paste and garlic in bowl; mix well. Combine 1 1/2 tablespoons of the sauce mixture with mushrooms; mix gently.

Place pitta bread on oven trays, spread with remaining sauce mixture. Top with spinach, mushroom mixture, cheeses and nuts. Bake, uncovered, in hot oven about 20 minutes or until topping is browned.

Per serve fat 12g; fibre 12g; kj 1616

wholemeal lentil
lasagne

cooking-oil spray

1¹/₂ cups (300g) brown lentils

1 teaspoon olive oil

2 cloves garlic, crushed

1 medium (150g) onion, chopped

1 medium (200g) red capsicum, chopped

200g button mushrooms, sliced

1 medium (120g) zucchini, chopped

1 teaspoon garam masala

2 teaspoons ground cumin

6 instant wholemeal lasagne sheets

2 cups (400g) low-fat ricotta cheese

¹/₄ cup (15g) stale breadcrumbs

¹/₂ cup (50g) grated low-fat mozzarella cheese

1 tablespoon chopped fresh parsley

Per serve fat 16g; fibre 17g; kj 2062

Coat 2 litre (8-cup) heatproof dish with cooking-oil spray.

Add lentils to large pan of boiling water, boil, uncovered, about 15 minutes or until tender; drain.

Heat oil in pan, add garlic and onion, cook, stirring, until onion is soft. Add capsicum, mushrooms, zucchini and spices, cook, stirring, until just tender; stir in lentils.

Cover base of the prepared dish with 3 lasagne sheets, spread with half the lentil mixture, then half the ricotta cheese. Repeat with remaining lasagne sheets, lentil mixture and ricotta cheese. Sprinkle with combined breadcrumbs, mozzarella cheese and parsley, bake, uncovered, in moderate oven about 45 minutes or until top is browned.

roast vegetables with
split pea sauce

800g pumpkin, chopped

1 medium (225g) swede, chopped

2 medium (250g) parsnips, chopped

2 large (360g) carrots, chopped

1 large (200g) onion, sliced

6 cloves garlic, peeled

1 tablespoon olive oil

1 tablespoon sumac

300g dried wheat noodles

2 tablespoons chopped fresh coriander leaves

split pea sauce

$1/2$ cup (100g) yellow split peas

3 cups (750ml) vegetable stock

1 small (80g) onion, chopped finely

2 cloves garlic, crushed

1 teaspoon ground cumin

1 teaspoon ground coriander

1 tablespoon lemon juice

$1/4$ cup (60ml) water

Toss vegetables with combined oil and sumac; place in single layer, in large non-stick baking dish. Bake, uncovered, in hot oven about 30 minutes or until browned and just tender. **Meanwhile**, cook noodles in large pan of boiling water, uncovered, until just tender; drain. Cover to keep warm. **Combine** vegetables in large bowl with noodles and coriander. Serve with hot Split Pea Sauce. **Split Pea Sauce** Rinse peas under cold water; drain. Combine peas, 2 cups (500ml) of the stock, onion and garlic in a large pan. Bring to boil; simmer, uncovered, 30 minutes or until peas are soft. Blend or process pea mixture with spices and remaining stock, juice and water. Return to pan and heat.

Per serve fat 8g; fibre 18g; kj 2310

chickpea

enchiladas

cooking-oil spray

8 x 20cm tortillas

1/2 small iceberg lettuce, shredded

2 x 425g cans chickpeas, rinsed, drained

3/4 cup (180ml) low-fat yogurt

1 cup (125g) grated low-fat cheddar cheese

4 green onions, chopped

tomato salsa

1 tablespoon water

1 medium (150g) onion, chopped

2 cloves garlic, crushed

1 medium (200g) green capsicum, chopped

4 small (520g) tomatoes, peeled, chopped

1/4 cup (60ml) tomato paste

1 bottled green jalapeno pepper, chopped

1 teaspoon ground hot paprika

1 teaspoon sugar

1/2 teaspoon dried crushed chillies

Microwave Tomato Salsa suitable

Per serve fat 15g; fibre 10g; kj 2386

Coat pan with cooking-oil spray, add tortillas, one at a time, cook on both sides until heated through and limp; use a little more spray on pan for each tortilla.

Top 4 tortillas with a small amount of lettuce, Tomato Salsa, chickpeas and yogurt, sprinkle with a little cheese. Fold tortillas in half, then quarters.

Top remaining tortillas with remaining lettuce, Tomato Salsa and chickpeas. Serve folded tortillas on flat tortillas. Sprinkle with remaining cheese; top with remaining yogurt and green onions.

Tomato Salsa

Combine water, onion and garlic in pan, cook, stirring, until onion is soft. Add remaining ingredients, simmer, uncovered, about 5 minutes or until thickened.

fennel and lentil
au gratin

1 cup (200g) brown lentils

2 large (1.3kg) fennel bulbs, quartered

1 tablespoon water

1 medium (150g) onion, chopped finely

2 cloves garlic, crushed

2 x 400g cans tomatoes

1 tablespoon chopped fresh oregano

1 tablespoon chopped fresh thyme

1 tablespoon chopped fresh basil leaves

1/2 cup (125ml) dry red wine

1 cup (70g) stale breadcrumbs

1/2 cup (40g) grated parmesan cheese

white sauce

30g butter

2 tablespoons plain flour

2 cups (500ml) skim milk

1/2 cup (60g) grated low-fat cheddar cheese

Add lentils to pan of boiling water, boil, uncovered, until tender; drain, rinse, drain. Add fennel to pan of boiling water, simmer, uncovered, 15 minutes or until tender; drain.

Combine water, onion and garlic in pan, cook until onion is soft. Add undrained crushed tomatoes, herbs and wine, simmer, uncovered, 15 minutes or until thick; stir in lentils.

Place half the lentil mixture in 2.5 litre (10-cup) heatproof dish, top with fennel and remaining lentil mixture. Pour over White Sauce, sprinkle with combined breadcrumbs and cheese. Bake, uncovered, in moderate oven 40 minutes or until lightly browned.

White Sauce Melt butter in pan, stir in flour, cook over heat until bubbling. Remove from heat, gradually stir in milk. Stir over heat until sauce boils and thickens, stir in cheese.

Per serve fat 13g; fibre 17g; kj 2003

minted ratatouille
lasagne

1 bunch (500) spinach, shredded

30g butter

1/2 cup (75g) plain flour

2 cloves garlic, crushed

3 cups (750ml) skim milk

8 instant lasagne pasta sheets

2 tablespoons stale breadcrumbs

ratatouille

1 medium (300g) eggplant, chopped

coarse cooking salt

2 teaspoons olive oil

2 medium (300g) onions, chopped

2 tablespoons plain flour

400g button mushrooms, sliced

1 medium (200g) green capsicum, chopped

2 x 400g cans tomatoes

2 tablespoons tomato paste

2 tablespoons chopped fresh mint leaves

2 teaspoons sugar

Boil, steam or microwave spinach until just wilted, rinse under cold water; drain. Squeeze excess moisture from spinach; chop finely. Melt butter in pan, add flour and garlic, cook, stirring, until mixture is dry and grainy. Remove from heat, gradually stir in milk. Stir over heat until mixture boils and thickens. Stir in spinach.

Spread one-third of Ratatouille over base of 2 litre (8-cup) heatproof dish. Top with 4 sheets of lasagne, then half the remaining Ratatouille and remaining lasagne sheets. Spread with remaining Ratatouille, then spinach sauce; sprinkle with breadcrumbs. Bake, uncovered, in moderately hot oven 30 minutes or until pasta is tender.

Ratatouille Place eggplant in colander, sprinkle with salt, stand 30 minutes. Rinse eggplant under cold water, drain on absorbent paper.

Heat oil in pan, add onions, cook, stirring, until onions are soft. Add flour, cook, stirring, until mixture is dry and grainy. Add eggplant, mushrooms, capsicum, undrained crushed tomatoes and paste, stir over heat until mixture boils and thickens. Simmer, uncovered, until mixture is thick and vegetables are soft. Stir in mint and sugar.

Microwave Sauce suitable
Per serve fat 11g; fibre 13g; kj 1905

kumara leek and sage
frittata

cooking-oil spray
2 medium (800g) kumara
1 small (200g) leek, sliced
1 clove garlic, crushed
1 tablespoon chopped fresh sage
3 eggs
3 egg whites
$1/2$ cup (125ml) skim milk
$1/3$ cup (40g) grated low-fat cheddar cheese
1 tablespoon chopped fresh parsley

Coat 25cm-round, 1.5 litre (6-cup) flan dish with cooking-oil spray. Cut kumara into 5mm slices. Boil, steam or microwave kumara until just tender; drain.

Heat non-stick pan, coat with cooking-oil spray, add leek and garlic, cook, covered, over low heat, stirring occasionally, until leek is soft. Stir in half the sage.

Place half the kumara slices over base of prepared dish, top with leek mixture, then remaining kumara. Pour combined eggs, egg whites, milk, cheese and parsley over kumara, sprinkle with remaining sage. Bake, uncovered, in moderate oven 35 minutes or until frittata is firm.

Microwave Kumara and leek suitable
Per serve fat 6g; fibre 4g; kj 962

sherried vegetable
hot pot with risoni

1.4kg butternut pumpkin, peeled

1 cup (250ml) vegetable stock

10 (400g) tiny new potatoes

2 teaspoons olive oil

1 teaspoon ground turmeric

1 teaspoon ground sweet paprika

1/2 cup (110g) risoni pasta

2 tablespoons water

1 large (500g) leek, chopped

5 cups (400g) shredded cabbage

2 cups (500ml) vegetable stock, extra

1/4 cup (60ml) dry sherry

1/4 cup chopped fresh chives

Chop pumpkin into 3cm pieces. Boil, steam or microwave half the pumpkin until tender, blend or process with stock until smooth; cool.

Place remaining pumpkin, potatoes, oil and spices in non-stick baking dish. Bake, uncovered, in moderately hot oven 1 hour or until vegetables are tender, stirring halfway through cooking.

Add risoni to pan of boiling water, simmer, uncovered, until tender, drain; cool.

Combine water and leek in large pan, cook, covered, over low heat, stirring occasionally, about 5 minutes or until leek is tender. Stir in cabbage, pumpkin puree, extra stock and sherry, simmer, uncovered, about 10 minutes or until cabbage is tender. Stir in potato mixture, risoni and chives, cook, stirring, until heated through.

Per serve fat 5g; fibre 13g; kj 1456

30 chickpeas with spinach and spices

2 tablespoons water

1 medium (150g) onion, chopped

3 cloves garlic, crushed

1 teaspoon ground cinnamon

1 teaspoon ground sweet paprika

2 teaspoons ground coriander

2 teaspoons cumin seeds

3 x 425g cans chickpeas, rinsed, drained

3 small (390g) tomatoes, chopped

2 tablespoons tomato paste

1/4 cup (40g) seeded chopped dates

1 cup (250ml) water, extra

1/4 cup chopped fresh coriander leaves

2 tablespoons chopped fresh mint

1 bunch (500g) spinach, chopped

Combine water, onion, garlic and spices in large pan, cook, stirring, until onion is soft. Stir in chickpeas, tomatoes, paste and dates; then extra water and herbs, simmer, covered, 10 minutes. Stir in spinach, simmer, uncovered, about 5 minutes or until spinach is just wilted.

Microwave Suitable
Per serve fat 5g; fibre 15g; kj 1078

polenta eggplant fritters

Cut 2 medium (600g) eggplant into 2cm slices. Place on flat surface, sprinkle with salt; stand 20 minutes. Rinse eggplant under cold water, dry on absorbent paper. Place 1/2 cup (75g) plain flour in small bowl. Combine 3/4 cup (125g) polenta and 3/4 cup (60g) grated parmesan cheese in another small bowl. Beat 3 eggs lightly in a third bowl. Coat eggplant in flour, dip in egg, coat in parmesan mixture. Shallow-fry eggplant in hot oil in large pan about 2 minutes each side or until browned and tender. Drain on absorbent paper.

Makes about 16

potato rosti

Combine 4 medium (800g) coarsely grated potatoes, 1 medium (150g) finely chopped onion and 80g melted butter in large bowl. Shallow-fry 1/4 cups of potato mixture in hot oil, until browned and crisp both sides. Drain on absorbent paper.

Makes about 12

grilled corn and red pepper fritters

Grill 2 (500g) cobs of corn, cut kernels off cobs; combine kernels, 1 1/4 cups (185g) self-raising flour, 1 lightly beaten egg and 1 small (150g) chopped red capsicum in large bowl. Stir in 2 cups (500ml) buttermilk. Pour by 1/3 cup (80ml) quantities into large heated oiled pan. Cook fritters until browned both sides and cooked through. Drain on absorbent paper.

Makes about 10

from left: potato rosti; polenta eggplant fritters; grilled corn and red pepper fritters; spiced chickpea and zucchini fritters.

spiced chickpea and zucchini fritters

Finely grate 2 large (300g) zucchini, squeeze out excess juice. Combine zucchini, 400g can drained chickpeas, 1 medium (150g) finely chopped onion and 1 clove crushed garlic in large bowl. Stir in 2 lightly beaten eggs, 1 cup (150g) plain flour, 2 teaspoons ground cumin, 1 teaspoon ground turmeric, 1 tablespoon finely chopped fresh coriander and 1/2 teaspoon ground cayenne pepper. Place mixture by heaped tablespoons, in heated oiled large pan. Flatten with spatula; cook fritters until browned both sides and cooked through. Drain on absorbent paper.

Makes about 15

**Cook about 3 medium (600g)
potatoes.**

$1/2$ cup (100g) dried pinto beans

$1/2$ cup (100g) dried red
kidney beans

2 teaspoons vegetable oil

1 large (200g) onion, sliced

1 litre (4 cups) vegetable stock

2 teaspoons Cajun seasoning

1 teaspoon ground cumin

1 medium (200g) red capsicum,
chopped

1 medium (200g) yellow capsicum,
chopped

2 (120g) baby eggplant, sliced

2 small (180g) zucchini, sliced

250g asparagus, chopped

150g green beans, chopped

1 cup (140g) frozen corn kernels

6 medium (1.1kg) tomatoes,
peeled, chopped

potato scones

$1^{1}/4$ cups (185g) self-raising flour

$1/4$ cup (40g) polenta

30g butter

1 tablespoon chopped fresh
basil leaves

$1/4$ cup (30g) grated low-fat
cheddar cheese

$1^{1}/4$ cups mashed potato

$1/4$ cup (60ml) skim milk

Per serve fat 13g; fibre 23g; kj 2636

potato scones

Cover dried pinto and kidney beans with cold water in large bowl; stand, covered, overnight. Drain.

Heat oil in 3 litre (12-cup) flameproof casserole dish, add onion, cook, stirring, until onion is soft. Add beans and stock, simmer, covered, 1 hour. Add remaining ingredients, simmer, covered, 5 minutes.

Top with Potato Scones, brush lightly with milk, bake, in moderate oven 35 minutes or until scones are browned.

Potato Scones
Combine flour and polenta in bowl, rub in butter. Stir in basil, cheese, potato and milk; mix to a soft dough. Turn dough onto floured surface, knead until smooth. Roll dough to 1.5cm thickness, cut into 4cm rounds.

chickpea, lentil and

bean soup

1 tablespoon water

1 large (300g) red onion, chopped

2 cloves garlic, crushed

1 teaspoon ground cumin

1 teaspoon ground turmeric

1 teaspoon ground sweet paprika

1/2 teaspoon ground cinnamon

2 x 425g cans chickpeas, rinsed, drained

300g can red kidney beans, rinsed, drained

1/2 cup (100g) red lentils

1.25 litres (5 cups) vegetable stock

1/4 cup (60ml) lemon juice

1/3 cup chopped fresh mint leaves

1 bunch (500g) spinach, shredded

Combine water, onion, garlic and spices in large pan, cook, stirring, until onion is soft. Add peas, beans, lentils, stock, juice and mint, simmer, covered, 20 minutes, stirring occasionally, or until lentils are soft.
Stir in spinach, simmer, uncovered, 5 minutes or until spinach is just wilted.

Freeze Suitable
Microwave Suitable
Per serve fat 5g; fibre 16g; kj 1179

vegetable and tofu
lasagne

1 tablespoon water

2 medium (300g) onions, chopped

2 cloves garlic, crushed

2 medium (240g) carrots, chopped

2 sticks celery, chopped

1 medium (200g) red capsicum, chopped

200g button mushrooms, chopped

6 medium (1.1kg) tomatoes, peeled, chopped

2 tablespoons tomato paste

1/4 cup chopped fresh basil leaves

1/4 cup chopped fresh parsley

3/4 cup (180ml) soft tofu

9 instant wholemeal lasagne pasta sheets

1/4 cup (15g) wholemeal stale breadcrumbs

1 tablespoon grated parmesan cheese

Combine water, onions, garlic, carrots, celery and capsicum in large non-stick pan; cook, stirring, 5 minutes or until onions are soft. Add mushrooms, cook, stirring, 1 minute. Add tomatoes, paste and herbs, simmer, covered, 15 minutes or until tender.

Beat tofu in small bowl until smooth, add 1/4 cup (60ml) of the tofu to vegetable mixture; mix well.

Spread a third of the vegetable mixture into greased 2 litre (8-cup), 20cm x 26cm heatproof dish. Top with 3 sheets of pasta. **Continue** layering vegetable mixture and pasta, finishing with pasta. Top with remaining tofu, then combined crumbs and cheese. Bake in moderate oven 50 minutes or until brown.

Per serve fat 3g; fibre 14g; kj 1005

roasted chilli vegetables
with **garlic** sauce

6 unpeeled cloves garlic

12 (500g) tiny new potatoes, halved

1 medium (200g) red capsicum, quartered

1 medium (200g) yellow capsicum, quartered

1 medium (200g) green capsicum, quartered

6 small (500g) onions, quartered

3 small (270g) zucchini, chopped

8 small (100g) yellow squash, halved

2 teaspoons olive oil

1¹/₂ tablespoons hot chilli sauce

2 teaspoons cracked black pepper

garlic sauce

2 cloves garlic, chopped

¹/₂ cup (125ml) sour light cream

1 tablespoon skim milk

¹/₄ cup firmly packed fresh basil leaves

2 teaspoons hot English mustard

1 tablespoon hot water

Combine garlic and vegetables with oil, sauce and pepper in large bowl; mix well. Spread vegetable mixture in single layers into two non-stick baking dishes.
Bake, uncovered, in moderate oven 40 minutes or until vegetables are tender, stirring twice during cooking. Serve with Garlic Sauce.
Garlic Sauce Blend or process all ingredients until smooth.

Per serve fat 10g; fibre 8g; kj 1065

40 baked mini
omelettes

cooking-oil spray

6 eggs

1 tablespoon skim milk

2 teaspoons plain flour

130g can creamed corn

2 cups (240g) frozen mixed vegetables, thawed, drained

1/4 teaspoon ground nutmeg

250g packet frozen spinach, thawed

Coat 4-holes (3/4cup/180ml) of Texas-style muffin pan with cooking-oil spray.
Whisk eggs, milk and flour together in bowl, stir in corn, vegetables and nutmeg. Squeeze excess moisture from spinach, stir into egg mixture. Pour mixture into prepared holes of pan
Bake in moderate oven 25 minutes or until set. Stand omelettes in pan 5 minutes before turning out.

Per serve fat 9g; fibre 8g; kj 770

lentil, vegetable and
brown rice pilaf

1 stick celery, chopped

1 medium (120g) carrot, chopped

1 medium (150g) onion, chopped

1 teaspoon ground cumin

2 teaspoons mild curry powder

1 teaspoon celery salt

1 cup (200g) brown lentils

1/2 cup (100g) brown rice

1 litre (4 cups) water

1 teaspoon grated fresh ginger

2 tablespoons chopped fresh parsley

Combine celery, carrot, onion, cumin, curry powder, salt, lentils, rice, water and ginger in medium pan, simmer, covered, 40 minutes or until rice is tender and water absorbed. Serve sprinkled with parsley.

Microwave Suitable
Per serve fat 2g; fibre 10g; kj 1031

42 stuffed baby
pumpkins

You will need to cook 1/3 cup (65g) long-grain rice for this recipe.

2 x 450g small golden nugget pumpkins
1 tablespoon water
1 medium (150g) onion, chopped finely
2 cloves garlic, crushed
2 teaspoons ground cumin
1 teaspoon ground coriander
2 teaspoons ground sweet paprika
1 teaspoon ground turmeric
3 small (390g) tomatoes, chopped finely
1 teaspoon sugar
1 cup cooked white rice
3/4 cup (110g) frozen broad beans, thawed, peeled
1 tablespoon chopped fresh coriander leaves

Cut tops from pumpkins and discard tops. Scoop out seeds and membranes from pumpkins, leaving 1cm thick shells.
Combine water, onion, garlic and spices in pan, cook, stirring, until onion is soft. Add tomatoes and sugar, simmer, uncovered, 10 minutes or until tomatoes are pulpy.
Combine tomato mixture with rice and beans; mix well. Spoon rice mixture into pumpkins; place in small baking dish. Bake, covered, in moderately hot oven about 1 1/2 hours or until pumpkins are tender. Serve cut in half, sprinkled with chopped fresh coriander.

Microwave Suitable
Per serve fat 1g; fibre 7g; kj 668

roasted pumpkin and
corn risotto

Chop pumpkin into 1.5cm pieces. Coat pumpkin with cooking-oil spray, add to baking dish, bake, uncovered, in very hot oven 35 minutes or until browned and tender.

Combine vegetable stock and tomato juice in large pan, bring to boil; cover, keep hot over low heat.

Combine water, onion and garlic in large heavy-based pan, cook, stirring, until onion is soft. Add rice, stir over heat 2 minutes. Add wine to pan, stir over low heat until liquid is absorbed. Stir in corn and 1/2 cup (125ml) of the stock mixture; cook, stirring, over low heat until liquid is absorbed.

Continue adding stock mixture gradually, stirring until absorbed before next addition. Total cooking time should be about 35 minutes or until rice is tender. Stir in roasted pumpkin, peas, cheese, parsley and pepper; stir until heated through.

2kg butternut pumpkin, peeled

cooking-oil spray

1.25 litres (5 cups) vegetable stock

850ml can tomato juice

1 tablespoon water

1 large (200g) onion, chopped finely

2 cloves garlic, crushed

2 cups (400g) arborio rice

1/2 cup (125ml) dry white wine

310g can corn kernels, drained

1 cup (125g) frozen peas, thawed

1/3 cup (25g) grated parmesan cheese

2 tablespoons chopped fresh parsley

1 teaspoon cracked black pepper

Per serve fat 7g;
fibre 13g; kj 2982

grilled haloumi,
tomato and rocket hokkien mee

14 large (1.3kg) egg tomatoes, halved lengthways

3 teaspoons olive oil

2 teaspoons balsamic vinegar

$1/2$ teaspoon salt

1 teaspoon cracked black pepper

1 bulb (45g) garlic, unpeeled

2 teaspoons balsamic vinegar, extra

$1/2$ cup (125ml) vegetable stock

600g Hokkien mee noodles

250g haloumi cheese

240g rocket, trimmed

Place tomatoes, cut side up, on wire rack over baking dish; drizzle with combined oil and vinegar, sprinkle with combined salt and pepper. Wrap garlic bulb in foil; place on rack with tomatoes. **Bake** tomatoes, uncovered, with garlic in moderate oven 1 hour. Cover tomatoes with foil, bake 30 minutes more. When garlic is cool enough to handle, peel; reserve pulp. Blend or process half the tomatoes with garlic pulp, extra vinegar and stock. **Meanwhile**, rinse noodles under hot water; drain. Transfer to large bowl and separate noodles with fork. Cut haloumi into 1cm slices; cook on heated oiled griddle pan until browned lightly on both sides. Just before serving, gently toss noodles in large bowl with pureed tomato mixture, remaining tomato halves, haloumi slices and torn rocket.

Per serve fat 16g; fibre 10g; kj 1796

ginger noodles

with vegetables

375g thick fresh egg noodles

2 medium (240g) carrots

2 medium (240g) zucchini

cooking-oil spray

1 medium (200g) red capsicum, chopped roughly

1 clove garlic, crushed

1 tablespoon grated fresh ginger

400g bok choy, shredded

425g can baby corn, drained, halved

2 tablespoons green ginger wine

2 tablespoons hoi sin sauce

1 tablespoon soy sauce

2 teaspoons cornflour

1 tablespoon water

Rinse noodles under cold water; drain. Using a vegetable peeler, peel long thin strips from carrots and zucchini. Heat wok or large pan, coat with cooking-oil spray, add carrots, zucchini, capsicum, garlic and ginger, stir-fry until carrots are just tender. Add bok choy and corn, stir-fry until bok choy is wilted. Add noodles, wine, sauces and blended cornflour and water, stir over heat until mixture boils and thickens slightly.

Per serve fat 3g; fibre 9g; kj 895

tofu and egg
salad

*2 teaspoons chopped
fresh coriander root*

1 clove garlic, crushed

*1 tablespoon grated
fresh ginger*

*2 tablespoons brown
sugar*

*2 tablespoons dark soy
sauce*

*1 teaspoon five-spice
powder*

*2 teaspoons vegetable
oil*

1/4 cup (60ml) water

*6 (about 200g)
radishes*

*375g firm tofu,
drained, cubed*

*1 tablespoon chopped
fresh coriander leaves*

*1 small fresh red chilli,
chopped finely*

*1 hard-boiled egg,
chopped*

Blend coriander root,
garlic, ginger, sugar,
sauce and five-spice
powder until well
combined. Heat oil in
pan, add blended
mixture, cook, stirring,
about 2 minutes or
until fragrant. Stir in
water; cool to room
temperature.

Cut radishes into thin
strips. Combine tofu
and radish in bowl,
pour over blended
mixture. Cover; stand
2 hours, stirring
occasionally. Just
before serving, drain
tofu mixture and
combine with chopped
fresh coriander, chilli
and egg.

Per serve fat 9g; fibre 1g;
kj 764

48 beans with tomatoes, fetta and olives

2 teaspoons olive oil

2 tablespoons pine nuts

400g green beans, halved

1 clove garlic, crushed

6 medium (450g) egg
tomatoes, chopped roughly

$^1/_2$ cup (60g) seeded black
olives

300g can red kidney beans,
rinsed, drained

2 tablespoons dry white wine

1 tablespoon lemon juice

2 teaspoons chopped
fresh thyme

2 teaspoons honey

150g reduced-fat fetta
cheese, cubed

Heat oil in wok or large pan,
add nuts, stir-fry until
browned; remove. Add green
beans and garlic to wok, stir-
fry 1 minute. Add tomatoes,
olives, kidney beans, wine,
juice, thyme and honey, stir-
fry until heated through. Stir
in nuts and cheese.

Per serve fat 14g; fibre 8g;
kj 1114

tomato
chilli lentils

2 teaspoons olive oil

1 clove garlic, crushed

1 teaspoon grated
fresh ginger

1 small fresh red chilli,
chopped finely

1 teaspoon garam
masala

2 medium (300g)
onions, sliced thinly

300g pumpkin,
chopped

2 (120g) baby
eggplant, chopped

150g button
mushrooms, halved

1 large (350g) red
capsicum, chopped

2 small (180g)
zucchini, chopped

3 x 400g cans
tomatoes

2 tablespoons seeded
mustard

1 tablespoon chopped
fresh parsley

3/4 cup (150g) red
lentils

Heat oil in large non-stick pan, add garlic, ginger, chilli, garam masala, onions, pumpkin and eggplant. Cook, stirring, until onions are soft. Add mushrooms, capsicum, zucchini and undrained crushed tomatoes; simmer, covered, 45 minutes. Stir in mustard, parsley and lentils, simmer, uncovered, for a further 25 minutes or until lentils are tender.

Per serve fat 5g; fibre 14g; kj 1099

spiced vegetables
with burghul

3 small (700g) eggplant

1 large (350g) red capsicum

2 medium (300g) onions

2 small (180g) zucchini

1 tablespoon water

2 cloves garlic, crushed

1 tablespoon ground cumin

1 tablespoon ground coriander

2 x 400g cans tomatoes

1 cinnamon stick

1 tablespoon lemon juice

1 tablespoon sugar

1/3 cup (55g) blanched almonds, toasted, chopped

burghul

1 cup (160g) burghul

20g butter, chopped

1/4 cup (35g) dried currants

Cut eggplant and capsicum into 2cm pieces, onions into wedges, zucchini into 1cm rounds.
Heat large non-stick pan, add water, eggplant, capsicum, onions, zucchini, garlic, cumin and coriander; cook, stirring, until onions are soft.
Add undrained crushed tomatoes, cinnamon and juice; simmer, covered, 45 minutes. Discard cinnamon stick, stir in sugar. Serve with Burghul and sprinkle with almonds.
Burghul Place burghul in heatproof bowl, cover with boiling water, stand 15 minutes. Rinse burghul under cold water; drain well, pat dry on absorbent paper. Add to heated pan, stir over low heat until burghul is dry; add butter and currants, stir gently until butter is melted.

Per serve fat 15g; fibre 19g; kj 1694

spicy vegetarian patties with
yogurt sauce

1 tablespoon water

1 medium (150g) onion, chopped finely

2 cloves garlic, crushed

1 medium (120g) carrot, grated

2 teaspoons ground cumin

1 tablespoon chopped fresh coriander leaves

2 tablespoons chopped fresh parsley

$1/4$ teaspoon sambal oelek

$1/3$ cup (80ml) bottled salsa

300g can chickpeas, rinsed, drained

150g firm tofu, drained, chopped

2 cups (140g) All-Bran

yogurt sauce

$1/3$ cup (80ml) low-fat yogurt

1 tablespoon shredded fresh mint leaves

Combine water, onion, garlic and carrot in medium non-stick pan, cook, stirring, until vegetables are soft. Add cumin, coriander, parsley, sambal oelek and salsa, cook, stirring, until fragrant.

Blend or process vegetable mixture, chickpeas, tofu and All-Bran until finely chopped. Cover; refrigerate several hours or until firm.

Shape chickpea mixture into 4 patties. Place patties on lightly greased oven tray. Bake in moderately hot oven 30 minutes; or until they are heated through.

Grill patties until browned both sides. Serve patties with Yogurt Sauce, or serve on toasted wholemeal rolls with salad, if desired.

Yogurt Sauce Combine yogurt and mint in bowl; mix well.

Microwave Vegetable mixture suitable
Per serve fat 9g; fibre 14g; kj 1357

54 hot 'n' spicy bean curd
on noodles

1kg fresh rice noodles

500g packet firm bean curd (tofu)

2 teaspoons peanut oil

2 cloves garlic, crushed

2 teaspoons finely grated fresh ginger

2 sticks celery, sliced thinly

2 medium (240g) carrots, sliced thinly

1 medium (200g) red capsicum, sliced thinly

6 green onions, sliced

1/2 cup (125ml) vegetable stock

1 tablespoon hot chilli sauce

1 tablespoon Chinese barbecue sauce

1/2 teaspoon sugar

1 teaspoon soy bean paste

2 teaspoons Chinese cooking wine

1 teaspoon cornflour

1 tablespoon water

Place noodles in bowl, cover with warm water, stand 5 minutes; drain. Cover to keep warm. Cut bean curd into 2cm pieces, place in heatproof bowl, cover with boiling water, stand 2 minutes; drain well.

Heat oil in wok or large pan, add garlic and ginger, stir-fry 1 minute. Add celery, carrots and capsicum, stir-fry until carrots are just tender.

Add onions, stock, sauces, sugar, paste, wine and blended cornflour and water, stir over heat until mixture boils and thickens. Add bean curd to pan, stir gently until heated through. Serve bean curd mixture on warm noodles.

Per serve fat 10g; fibre 7g; kj 1923

vegetarian
shepherd's pie

cooking-oil spray

*2 medium (300g)
onions, sliced*

*2 cloves garlic,
crushed*

*1 tablespoon mild
curry powder*

*2 x 400g cans
tomatoes*

*3 cups (300g)
chopped cauliflower*

*3¹/₂ cups (300g)
chopped broccoli*

*2 medium (240g)
carrots, sliced*

*2 medium (250g)
parsnips, sliced*

*2 tablespoons mild
sweet chilli sauce*

potato topping

*6 medium (1.2kg)
potatoes, peeled*

*2 tablespoons sour
light cream*

20g butter

Microwave Potatoes
suitable
Per serve fat 9g;
fibre 17g; kj 1606

Heat non-stick pan, coat with cooking-oil spray,
add onions and garlic, cook, stirring, until
onions are soft. Add curry powder, cook,
stirring, until fragrant.

Add undrained crushed tomatoes and
remaining ingredients, simmer, uncovered,
10 minutes or until vegetables are tender and
mixture has thickened; cool 10 minutes.

Spoon vegetable mixture into 2.5 litre (10-cup)
heatproof dish, spread with Potato Topping.
Bake in moderately hot oven 25 minutes or until
browned and hot.

Potato Topping Boil, steam or microwave
potatoes until tender; drain. Mash potatoes with
cream and butter.

pumpkin and leek

soup

500g pumpkin

1 large (300g) potato, chopped

$1/4$ teaspoon ground turmeric

$1/4$ teaspoon garam masala

2 tablespoons water

1 medium (350g) leek, chopped

1 stick celery, chopped

1 large vegetable stock cube

2 cups (500ml) water, extra

2 tablespoons chopped fresh parsley

Cut pumpkin into 1cm cubes. Boil, steam or microwave half the pumpkin with the potato until soft, drain; mash well.

Add spices to dry pan, cook, stirring, until fragrant. Add water, leek and celery, cook, stirring, until leek is soft. Add chopped raw pumpkin, crumbled stock cube, extra water and mashed vegetables to pan, simmer, covered, 5 minutes, or until pumpkin is tender. Stir in parsley.

Freeze Suitable
Microwave Suitable
Per serve fat 1g; fibre 4g; kj 460

eggplant with pumpkin and fetta

You will need to cook ⅓ cup (65g) long-grain rice for this recipe.

4 medium (1.2kg) eggplant, halved lengthways

coarse cooking salt

cooking-oil spray

200g piece pumpkin, chopped finely

1 small (80g) onion, chopped finely

2 cloves garlic, crushed

1 teaspoon ground cumin

2 tablespoons brown sugar

1 cup cooked white rice

2 tablespoons chopped fresh coriander leaves

⅓ cup (50g) hazelnuts, toasted, chopped

100g reduced-fat fetta cheese, crumbled

Per serve fat 13g; fibre 10g; kj 1291

Sprinkle cut side of eggplant with salt, stand 30 minutes. Rinse under cold water, pat dry with absorbent paper. Coat cut surfaces of eggplant with cooking-oil spray, place on wire rack over baking dish.

Bake, uncovered, in moderate oven 40 minutes or until eggplant are tender, cool 10 minutes. Scoop flesh from eggplant, leaving 5mm shells. Chop eggplant flesh.

Coat heated non-stick pan with cooking-oil spray, add pumpkin, onion, garlic and cumin, cook, stirring, until pumpkin is just tender. Stir in eggplant flesh, sugar, rice, coriander and nuts.

Divide pumpkin mixture among eggplant shells, place on oven tray; top with cheese. Bake, uncovered, in moderate oven 30 minutes or until cheese is lightly browned.

58 vegetable cheese
puffs

cooking-oil spray

2 teaspoons vegetable oil

60g pumpkin, chopped finely

1 small (100g) red onion, chopped

1/2 small (40g) carrot, grated

1/4 small (40g) red capsicum, chopped

1/2 small (50g) zucchini, grated

15g butter

1 tablespoon plain flour

1/3 cup (80ml) skim milk

1/4 cup (20g) grated parmesan cheese

2 eggs, separated

1 egg white

Coat four ³/₄-cup (180ml) souffle dishes with cooking-oil spray. Heat oil in non-stick pan, add vegetables, cover, cook until pumpkin is tender. Process vegetables until combined. Melt butter in medium pan, stir in flour; cook over heat until bubbling. Remove from heat, gradually stir in milk. Stir over heat until mixture boils and thickens, remove from heat, stir in vegetable mixture, cheese and egg yolks.

Beat the 3 egg whites in small bowl with electric mixer until soft peaks form, fold into vegetable mixture in 2 batches. Spoon mixture into prepared dishes, place on oven tray. Bake in hot oven 10 minutes, reduce heat to moderate, bake further 15 minutes or until browned and puffed. Serve immediately.

Per serve fat 11g; fibre 1g; kj 643

glossary

all-bran a low-fat, high-fibre breakfast cereal based on wheat bran.

beans
broad beans (fava beans): available fresh, frozen and dried.
green: sometimes called French beans.
mix (4-bean mix): a canned mix of red kidney, garbanzo, baby lima and butter beans.

black bean sauce made from fermented soy beans, spices, water and flour.

bok choy also called pak choi or Chinese cabbage.

breadcrumbs
packaged: fine-textured, crunchy, purchased white breadcrumbs.
stale: one- or two-day-old bread made into crumbs by grating, blending or processing.

butter 125g is equal to 1 stick butter.

cajun seasoning can include paprika, basil, onion, fennel, thyme, cayenne and tarragon.

capsicum also known as bell pepper or, simply, pepper.

cheese
haloumi: a firm, cream-coloured sheep milk cheese.
light cream: the version of Philadelphia with 30% less fat than the regular version.
low-fat cheddar: we used one with a fat content of not more than 7%.

low-fat mozzarella: we used Reduced Fat Mozzarella Cheese by Kraft Light Naturals.
low-fat ricotta: a low-fat, fresh, unripened cheese made from whey obtained in the manufacture of other cheese.
reduced-fat fetta: we used a fetta with an average fat content of 15%.
smoked: we used a firm smoked cheese.

chinese barbecue sauce a thick, sweet and salty commercial sauce used in marinades; made from fermented soy beans, vinegar, garlic, pepper and various spices. Available from Asian specialty stores.

coriander also known as cilantro or Chinese parsley; bright-green-leafed herb with a pungent flavour. Often stirred into a dish just before serving.

cornflour also known as cornstarch.

cream, light sour (minimum fat content 18%): a less dense, commercially cultured soured cream.

eggplant also known as aubergine.

fillo pastry also known as phyllo dough; comes in tissue-thin pastry sheets bought chilled or frozen.

five-spice powder a fragrant mixture of ground cloves, fennel seeds, cinnamon, star anise and Sichuan pepper.

garam masala a powdered blend of spices based on cardamom, cinnamon, clove, coriander and cumin. Sometimes chilli is added, making a hot variation.

green ginger wine alcoholic sweet wine infused with finely ground ginger.

hoisin sauce a thick, sweet and spicy Chinese paste made from salted fermented soy beans, onions and garlic.

jalapeno pepper fairly hot green chillies, available in brine bottled or fresh from specialty greengrocers.

kumara orange-fleshed sweet potato.

lebanese cucumber short and stocky, this variety also known as the European or burpless cucumber.

milk, skim we used milk with 0.1% fat content.

mixed herbs, dried a blend of dried, crushed thyme, rosemary, marjoram, basil, oregano and sage.

mushrooms
button: small, cultivated white mushrooms having a delicate, subtle flavour.
chinese dried: also known as dried shiitake mushrooms; have a meaty flavour.

noodles
dried wheat: fine noodles made from wheat flour, salt and water.
fresh egg: made from wheat flour and eggs; strands vary in thickness.

fresh rice: thick, wide, almost white in colour; made from rice and vegetable oil. Must be covered with boiling water before using.

hokkien mee: fresh wheat noodles.

oil

cooking-oil spray: vegetable oil in an aerosol can, available in supermarkets.

olive: a mono-unsaturated oil, made from the pressing of tree-ripened olives; especially good for everyday cooking and in salad dressings. Light describes the mild flavour, not the fat levels.

peanut: pressed from ground peanuts; most commonly used oil in Asian cooking because of its high smoke point.

sesame: made from roasted, crushed, white sesame seeds; a flavouring rather than a cooking medium.

vegetable: any of a number of oils sourced from plants rather than animal fats.

pepitas dried pumpkin seeds.

pizza sauce a blend of tomato paste, herbs and spices.

risoni pasta rice-shaped pasta, also known as orzo.

rocket a green salad leaf.

salsa, bottled a combination of tomatoes, onions, peppers, vinegar, herbs and spices.

sambal oelek (also ulek or olek) a salty paste made from ground chillies, sugar and spices.

snow peas also called mange tout ("eat all").

soy bean paste made from cooked, mashed, salted and fermented soy beans.

spinach

English: correct name for spinach; the green vegetable often called spinach is correctly known as Swiss chard, silverbeet or seakale. Delicate, crinkled green leaves on thin stems; high in iron, it's good eaten raw in salads or steamed gently on its own.

sugar snap peas small pods with small, formed peas inside; they are eaten whole, cooked or uncooked.

sumac a purple-red, astringent spice ground from berries growing on shrubs that flourish wild around the Mediterranean. Especially good in salad dressings and sauces.

tamarind concentrate a thick, purple-black, ready-to-use sweet/sour paste extracted from the pulp of pods from tamarind trees; use as is, with no soaking.

tofu also known as beancurd, an off-white, custard-like product made from the "milk" of crushed soy beans; comes fresh as firm or silken, and processed as fried or pressed dried sheets.

tomato pasta sauce, bottled prepared sauce available from supermarkets.

tortilla thin, round unleavened bread originating in Mexico; can be made at home or purchased frozen, fresh or vacuum-packed. Two kinds are available, one made from wheat flour and the other from corn (maizemeal).

vegetable stock cube contains no animal products but is salty to taste; 1 cube is equivalent to 2 teaspoons powdered bouillon. If you prefer to make your own fresh stock, see recipe on page 3.

yeast a 7g ($^{1}/_{4}$oz) sachet of dried yeast (2 teaspoons) is equal to 15g ($^{1}/_{2}$oz) compressed yeast if substituting one for the other.

yogurt, low fat, plain we used yogurt with a fat content of less than 0.2%.

zucchini also known as courgette.

facts and figures

These conversions are approximate only, but the difference between an exact and the approximate conversion of various liquid and dry measures is minimal and will not affect your cooking results.

Measuring equipment

The difference between one country's measuring cups and another's is, at most, within a 2 or 3 teaspoon variance. (For the record, 1 Australian metric measuring cup holds approximately 250ml.) The most accurate way of measuring dry ingredients is to weigh them. For liquids, use a clear glass or plastic jug having metric markings.

Note: NZ, Canada, USA and UK all use 15ml tablespoons. Australian tablespoons measure 20ml.
All cup and spoon measurements are level.

How to measure

When using graduated measuring cups, shake dry ingredients loosely into the appropriate cup. Do not tap the cup on a bench or tightly pack the ingredients unless directed to do so. Level the top of measuring cups and measuring spoons with a knife. When measuring liquids, place a clear glass or plastic jug having metric markings on a flat surface to check accuracy at eye level.

Dry Measures

metric	imperial
15g	1/2oz
30g	1oz
60g	2oz
90g	3oz
125g	4oz (1/4lb)
155g	5oz
185g	6oz
220g	7oz
250g	8oz (1/2lb)
280g	9oz
315g	10oz
345g	11oz
375g	12oz (3/4lb)
410g	13oz
440g	14oz
470g	15oz
500g	16oz (1lb)
750g	24oz (11/2lb)
1kg	32oz (2lb)

We use large eggs having an average weight of 60g.

Liquid Measures

metric	imperial
30ml	1 fluid oz
60ml	2 fluid oz
100ml	3 fluid oz
125ml	4 fluid oz
150ml	5 fluid oz (1/4 pint/1 gill)
190ml	6 fluid oz
250ml (1cup)	8 fluid oz
300ml	10 fluid oz (1/2 pint)
500ml	16 fluid oz
600ml	20 fluid oz (1 pint)
1000ml (1litre)	13/4 pints

Helpful Measures

metric	imperial
3mm	1/8in
6mm	1/4in
1cm	1/2in
2cm	3/4in
2.5cm	1in
6cm	21/2in
8cm	3in
20cm	8in
23cm	9in
25cm	10in
30cm	12in (1ft)

Oven Temperatures

These oven temperatures are only a guide.
Always check the manufacturer's manual.

	C°(Celsius)	F°(Fahrenheit)	Gas Mark
Very slow	120	250	1
Slow	150	300	2
Moderately slow	160	325	3
Moderate	180–190	350–375	4
Moderately hot	200–210	400–425	5
Hot	220–230	450–475	6
Very hot	240–250	500–525	7

Food editor Pamela Clark
Associate food editor Karen Hammial
Assistant food editor Kathy McGarry
Assistant recipe editor Elizabeth Hooper
Home Library Staff
Editor-in-chief Mary Coleman
Marketing manager Nicole Pizanis
Designer Jackie Richards
Group publisher Paul Dykzeul
Produced by The Australian Women's Weekly Home Library, Sydney.
Colour separations by ACP Colour Graphics Pty Ltd, Sydney.
Printing by Diamond Press Pty Ltd, Sydney.
Published by ACP Publishing Pty Limited, 54 Park St, Sydney;
GPO Box 4088, Sydney, NSW 1028. Ph: (02) 9282 8618 Fax: (02) 9267 9438.
AWWHomeLib@publishing.acp.com.au
Australia: Distributed by Network Distribution Company,
GPO Box 4088, Sydney, NSW 1028. Ph: (02) 9282 8777 Fax: (02) 9264 3278.
United Kingdom: Distributed by Australian Consolidated Press (UK),
Moulton Park Business Centre, Red House Rd, Moulton Park, Northampton, NN3 6AQ.
Ph: (01604) 497 531 Fax: (01604) 497 533 Acpukltd@aol.com
Canada: Distributed by Whitecap Books Ltd,
351 Lynn Ave, North Vancouver, BC, V7J 2C4 (604) 980 9852.
New Zealand: Distributed by Netlink Distribution Company,
17B Hargreaves St, Level 5, College Hill, Auckland 1, (9) 302 7616.
South Africa: Distributed by Intermag,
PO Box 57394, Springfield 2137 Johannesburg, SA, (011) 491 7534.

Healthy Eating: Vegetarian

Includes index.
ISBN 1 86396 095 3

1. Vegetarian cookery. I. Title: Australian Women's Weekly.
(Series: Australian Women's Weekly Home Library).
641.5636

ACP Publishing Pty Limited 1998
ACN 053 273 546

Cover: Spinach, Potato and Fetta Cheese Pie, page 17.
Stylist Vicki Liley **Photographer** Scott Cameron
Plates from Country Road
Back cover: Capsicum Casserole with Zucchini and Beans, page 4.